BOOK

OF THE

FOUNDING FATHERS

☆

VINCENT WILSON, JR

American History Research Associates
Brookeville, Maryland

Printed in the United States of America
by
R. R. Donnelley & Sons Company
Harrisonburg, Virginia

Fifth Printing - 2003

ISBN 0-910086-01-X

LIBRARY OF CONGRESS CATALOG CARD NO. 74-78128

American History Research Associates

BOX 140, BROOKEVILLE, MARYLAND

CONTENTS

"Sir, I agree to this Constitution, with all its faults, if they are such; because I think a general government necessary for us, and there is no form of government but what may be a blessing to the people if well administered; and I believe farther that this is likely to be well administered for a course of years, and can only end in despotism as other forms have done before it, when the people shall become so corrupted as to need despotic government, being incapable of any other."

—Benjamin Franklin
Address to the Constitutional Convention

INTRODUCTION

The Founding Fathers created an independent nation and gave shape and substance to the system of government that has endured longer than any other democracy in the history of the world. Some of the credit for this 200-year record must inevitably go to those who kept it going, but those who risked so much to make this an independent nation and those who created and initiated the American system of government must always hold a special place in the shrine of American heroes.

The Founding Fathers came from no single mold: most were men of property, a few very rich. Lawyers, doctors, merchants, soldiers, printers, scientists, farmers and planters — they were men of achievement; men who had put to good use the freedom and independence that they had enjoyed and refused to relinquish; active men who won their place in the New World by their own industry and merit (except for a few who inherited wealth); men who, having tasted tyranny, valued freedom and yet recognized the importance of law — and of limited power in a government; men who could finally agree that the ultimate power of the state should repose, not in any man or body of men, but in a body of laws — the Constitution.

The Founding Fathers faced a combination of challenges and opportunities unique in human history. In the eighteenth century, in a world where kings and queens exercised almost absolute power of life and death over their subjects, they dared challenge such power, and, once successful, they went on to create as perfect a governmental system as they could, and then proceeded to make it work.

Some of the leaders clearly revealed that they appreciated the exceptional nature of the opportunity before them. At the Philadelphia Convention in 1787, George Mason wrote, "The eyes of the United States are turned upon this assembly," and Madison: "The whole community is big with expectation, and there can be no doubt but that the result will in some way or other have a powerful effect on our destiny."

There is, of course, no definitive listing of Founding Fathers, although those who signed such important documents as the Declaration of Independence and the Constitution are generally recognized as candidates. But there are others — like Patrick Henry, George Mason and John Marshall, who did not sign either document — who contributed immensely to the founding of the United States; whereas some signers of those documents contributed little more than their signatures. All of the signers are listed in the back of the book, but this book features those men who made the most significant contributions to the founding of the nation — those who conceived and promoted the idea of independence from Britain, those who dared to think in terms of a single new nation, those who created a unique governmental system expressly for the new nation, and those who translated this new system into the first federal democracy in the world.

A few men — giants like Washington, Adams, Jefferson, Madison, Franklin and Hamilton — made monumental contributions at almost every phase of development, from the first stages of revolution to the establishment of a settled national government. These six men stand alone, for without their achievements, it is difficult to conceive of events developing as they did — Washington, the cool, steadfast military and political leader; Adams, the champion of independence, the diplomat; Jefferson, the philosopher-statesman, diplomat and political leader; Madison, the Father of the Constitution and the Bill of Rights, author of The Federalist Papers; Hamilton, the brilliant military aide, the originator of the national financial system, author of The Federalist Papers; and Franklin, the wise diplomat who won French help for the Revolution and helped bring the Convention to accept the Constitution. And four of the six, as the first four Presidents, guided the nation through its first quarter century.

However great the accomplishments of the Founding Fathers, it is well for us to remember that these men were neither gods nor demi-gods, no matter how much the giant statues erected in their honor may suggest that they were. Unfortunately, towering statues distort history, for such monumental dimensions may awe the beholder, creating the impression that these men were a race apart.

These men were great precisely because they were at times able to rise above their own interests and serve a larger cause. But Washington was known to be hungry for land, Hancock vain, Hamilton ambitious, Adams quarrelsome, Jefferson vindictive, and Henry tyrannical. Some were committed deeply to the ideals of the rights of man, but most were realistic in their expectations of man's acts. Certainly the Constitution, with its carefully balanced, separate-but-equal branches of government, is based on the assumption that the individual in office tends to misuse power; no man, therefore, should have too much. And the Bill of Rights is based on essentially the same assumption — that men and governments tend to misuse power, and therefore the individual must be guaranteed protection from both.

Not all of the Founding Fathers believed that the new nation should be dedicated to the principle that "all men . . . are endowed by their Creator with certain unalienable rights, that among these are life, liberty and the pursuit of happiness." Most of the men from Georgia and the Carolinas considered slavery a normal part of their way of life, and they had no intention of changing it. A few men from Southern States, such as George Mason and Thomas Jefferson, though products of plantation life themselves, were among the first to denounce slavery. But it is important to note that the matter of slavery was not dealt with directly in the U.S. Constitution. At the Constitutional Convention, George Mason, Gouverneur Morris, Elbridge Gerry and others denounced slavery as immoral and inhuman, but the representatives from Southern States threatened not to join the Union if the Constitution contained provisions against their "interest." The best that those against slavery could do was to establish a fixed date (1808) after which the importation of slaves would be prohibited. From the start, therefore, the country had to compromise on the slavery issue to achieve "Union."

In spite of such compromises, the Founding Fathers managed to create a system that has proved flexible and durable enough to remain effective through industrial and technological revolutions and world wars that have destroyed or rendered obsolete many other forms of government. Perhaps the ultimate testimonial to the Founding Fathers of the first modern republic — besides the existence of the United States itself — is the number of republics in the world today.

JOHN ADAMS
of
Massachusetts

Like the great Virginians — Washington, Jefferson and Madison — John Adams was one of the towering figures of the American Revolution; like them, he was a principal character in almost every act of that great drama: he was a leader of the movement for independence; he helped draft and signed the Declaration of Independence; he nominated Washington to lead the American forces; he won recognition and support for the struggling nation from the courts of Europe; he served as peace commissioner, and then, as Vice-President and President, helped direct the infant nation during its early years. Like them, he gave shape and substance to the ideas of liberty and independence, helping translate these into the institutions and practices of a new kind of government.

An outspoken patriot, Adams early embraced the idea of independence — in newspaper articles and pamphlets, in publications such as his *Thoughts on Government* (1776), and at the Continental Congress, where he argued forcefully for total independence from Britain, finally winning reluctant members to approve the Declaration that he helped draft. Regarding the Declaration, Jefferson said that Adams was "the pillar of its support on the floor of Congress," and Stockton of New Jersey called Adams "the Atlas of American independence." And it was Adams who in 1777 conceived the pattern for the flag that became the emblem of the new nation.

During the war he served in Congress on the Board of War and many important committees, and represented America first in the Netherlands, where, after lengthy diplomatic maneuvering, he obtained recognition and a substantial loan, and then in France, where he helped negotiate the peace treaty with Britain. After the war he was instrumental in obtaining important trade treaties with European countries, and as the first U.S. Minister to England, he undertook the delicate diplomatic task of establishing friendly relations with the former enemy. In London he helped resolve some of the problems that remained unsettled after the war, but he was severely hampered by a weak and divided Congress at home.

The selection of Adams as Vice-President and President testify to the place he won for himself by his years of service, his ability, and his commitment to the founding of the republic. Not a natural leader or heroic figure, he yet was raised to the highest offices in the land. Succeeding the powerful figure of Washington would have been difficult for any man, and Adams's administration was clouded with the beginnings of party strife. But it was fitting that he should have the opportunity to direct the fortunes of the nation he had done so much to build.

BY ASHER DURAND

1735	Born Oct. 30 Braintree, Mass.
1755	Graduated from Harvard
1758	Admitted to the bar
1774–78	Member, Continental Congress
1778–79	U.S. Commissioner to France
1779	Drafted Massachusetts constitution
1780–81	U.S. Minister to the Netherlands
1782–83	U.S. Peace Commissioner in France
1785–88	U.S. Minister to Great Britain
1789–97	Vice-President of the United States
1797–1801	President of the United States
1826	Died Jul. 4 Quincy, Mass.

SAMUEL ADAMS
of
Massachusetts

A political activist and patriot without peer, Sam Adams was one of the leading architects of the American Revolution: with remarkable singleness of purpose, this cousin of John Adams devoted himself to the cause of independence, largely neglecting his own interests. In articles and speeches he denounced British tyranny, and he led his patriotic followers to such political acts as the Boston "Massacre" and the Boston Tea Party. The first to question the British right to tax the colonies, he dared to be identified as a rebel leader — and he was the one, along with John Hancock, that British troops were after when they came to Lexington on April 19, 1775.

In 1765 Adams openly encouraged citizens to defy the Stamp Act, and he was the prime mover behind the meeting of all the colonies at the Stamp Act Congress in New York.

Adams worked against the British as a member of the Massachusetts legislature, in the powerful position of clerk, and less openly as founder of the Massachusetts committee of correspondence and a leader of the secret society, the Sons of Liberty. This patriotic — and radical — group resorted to violence and demonstrations on several occasions, storming the Governor's home and hanging the British tax collector in effigy.

On March 5, 1770, a group of colonists threatened British soldiers in Boston, precipitating an incident in which three colonists were killed. Adams and Joseph Warren called it the Boston "Massacre," and news of the "massacre" helped promote anti-British feeling.

Adams helped create another incident in December 1773, when the Sons of Liberty, encouraged by Adams, boarded British ships and dumped hundreds of chests of tea overboard — to protest the tax on tea. Adams had a genius for the daring act that would strike political flint.

Adams attended the First Continental Congress in 1774, and, on April 18, 1775, he was with Hancock in Lexington, about to go to the Second Congress, when Paul Revere arrived with news that British troops were after them — and they rode off early on the 19th, before the troops arrived, and those first shots were fired.

Although Sam Adams served in Congress until 1781 and held high government positions after the war, his great passion was independence, and once that was gained, he had completed his quest. After he signed the Declaration of Independence, he wrote that it "should have been made immediately after April 19, 1775."

In his search for freedom and independence Sam Adams was ever impatient, but he had the will and the ability to shape events that helped make independence in America a reality in his own time.

1722	Born Sept. 27 Boston, Mass.
1740	Graduated from Harvard
1756	Tax Collector in Boston
1765	Member, Massachusetts legislature
1766–74	Clerk, Massachusetts legislature
1772	Founder of Massachusetts Committee of Correspondence
1773	Organized Boston Tea Party
1774–81	Member, Continental Congress
1781–88	President, Massachusetts Senate
1789–93	Lt. Governor of Massachusetts
1794–97	Governor of Massachusetts
1803	Died Oct. 2 Boston, Mass.

CHARLES CARROLL
of
Maryland

One of the largest landholders in America, Charles Carroll was a leader of the Catholic community in Maryland and the only Catholic to sign the Declaration of Independence. Like Washington and Hancock, he risked a great fortune by defying the mother country.

After years of study in Europe, Carroll returned to a country indignant over new British taxation, especially the Stamp Act. Although as a Catholic he was unable to hold office, he became a leader of the opposition — partly through newspaper articles he wrote under a pen-name. He was a member of the colony's committee of observation, a group directing activities of patriots; the provincial committee of correspondence; and Maryland's unofficial legislature. He actively supported the policy of non-importation of British goods.

In 1776 Congress appointed Carroll; his cousin John, one of the leading American Jesuits; Samuel Chase; and Benjamin Franklin commissioners to Canada — to try to bring Canada into the struggle on the side of the colonies. However, American troops had already invaded Canada, turning the French Canadians against the American cause. The mission failed.

Carroll returned from Canada in June 1776, in time to take a firm stand for independence in the Maryland legislature, and after helping win the legislature's approval, he was selected as a delegate to the Continental Congress, where he signed the Declaration of Independence.

For the next twenty-five years, Carroll played a prominent part in both State and national affairs. In Congress during the war, he served with the Board of War and other important committees.

A champion of freedom of religion, Carroll contributed to the Maryland constitution, and though he declined to attend the Constitutional Convention, he supported the U.S. Constitution. As one of Maryland's Senators in the First U.S. Congress, he was instrumental in bringing Rhode Island, which had not ratified the U.S. Constitution, into the Union, and he assisted in drafting the amendments to the Constitution known as the Bill of Rights, finally assuring the freedom of worship and other freedoms for which he had risked so much.

When Carroll died in 1832 he was reputed to be the wealthiest man in America — and the last surviving signer of the Declaration of Independence.

BY REMBRANDT PEALE

1737   Born Sept. 20   Annapolis, Md.

1745–57   Studied in France

1757–64   Studied law in England

1775–76   Member, Maryland Convention

1776   Commissioner to Canada

1776–78   Member, Continental Congress

1777–1804   Member, Maryland Senate

1787   Elected delegate to Constitutional
         Convention; declined

1789–92   U.S. Senator

1832   Died Nov. 14   Baltimore, Md.

SAMUEL CHASE
of
Maryland

Like Samuel Adams and Patrick Henry, Samuel Chase was a political activist: his daring speeches against British tyranny stirred fellow Marylanders as well as members of the Continental Congress to support the cause of independence.

Of powerful build and persuasive manner, Chase won a position of leadership in the Maryland colonial legislature while in his twenties. He vigorously opposed the Stamp Act and helped establish the patriotic committee of correspondence in Maryland.

At the Continental Congress he was one of the first to speak out for independence. Early in 1776 he went to Canada as a Congressional commissioner — with Benjamin Franklin, and John and Charles Carroll — to try to persuade the French-Canadians to join in fighting the British, but the mission was unsuccessful. Chase returned to Philadelphia in time to learn of Lee's resolution on independence, introduced June 7th, but at that time the Maryland delegates were not authorized to vote for independence. Chase left Philadelphia and made a special trip through Maryland to win the people's support, and before the end of June the Maryland Convention voted for independence — and its delegates in Philadelphia were authorized to sign the Declaration of Independence.

After the war Chase was against the idea of a national government and refused to attend the Constitutional Convention, but by the 1790s he was identified with the Federalist party, and President Washington appointed him to the U.S. Supreme Court. As an associate justice, Chase became known for his positive, often impressive opinions, some of which provided an enduring base for the new judicial system. But he was on occasion too much the loyal Federalist: he strongly supported the sedition laws, passed during the Adams' administration, which prohibited political opposition to the Government, and which Jefferson and his fellow Democrat-Republicans saw as an abridgement of the First Amendment.

In 1804, after Chase had uttered some exceedingly intemperate remarks, the House of Representatives initiated impeachment action, but the Senate did not find him guilty. He remained in office, although he was in later years overshadowed by the new Chief Justice, John Marshall. But he had already made a substantial contribution to the U.S. judicial system — and gained the dubious distinction of being the only Founding Father to undergo impeachment proceedings.

BY CHARLES PEALE   MARYLAND HISTORICAL SOCIETY

1741 Born Apr. 17 Somerset County, Md.

1761 Admitted to the bar

1764–84 Member, Maryland legislature

1774–78 Member, Continental Congress

1776 Commissioner to Canada

1788 Member, Maryland Ratification Convention

1788–91 Judge, Criminal Court, Baltimore

1791–95 Chief Judge, Maryland General Court

1796–1811 Associate Justice, U.S. Supreme Court

1811 Died Jun. 19 Baltimore, Md.

GEORGE CLYMER

of

Pennsylvania

George Clymer was a wealthy Philadelphia businessman and banker who emerged as a leader of the patriots in the early 1770s, served in public office for over twenty years, and signed both the Declaration of Independence and the U.S. Constitution. A man of unusual intellectual curiosity, he also served as an officer of the Philadelphia Academy of Fine Arts and the Philadelphia Agricultural Society.

One of the first members of Pennsylvania's committee of safety, and one of the first to advocate complete independence from Britain, Clymer was called upon by the Continental Congress to serve as the first treasurer for the United Colonies, and he undertook the almost impossible assignment of raising money to support the government's operations, chief of which was the new Continental Army. And Clymer devoted not only his great energy, but also his own fortune to the cause, exchanging all his money, which was in hard coin, for the shaky continental currency.

In late 1776, when Congress fled a threatened Philadelphia, Clymer was one of the committee of three (with Robert Morris and George Walton) left behind to maintain essential government activities. During this crisis Clymer drove himself almost to a state of exhaustion, and he was forced to take a complete rest. Shortly after he recovered, the British captured Philadelphia and plundered and destroyed his home.

In Congress, Clymer performed valuable services as a member of committees dealing with financial matters. During the final years of the war, he was again responsible for obtaining funds for the Army.

At the Constitutional Convention Clymer, who was not an exceptional speaker, distinguished himself by his work in committees dealing with his specialty — finance.

In 1791, after a term in the First Congress, Clymer served as Federal Collector of the controversial tax on liquor which led to the Whiskey Rebellion. He concluded his career by negotiating an equitable peace treaty between the United States and the Creek tribe in Georgia.

A man of wealth who literally risked his fortune on the revolution, and whose home was destroyed by the British, Clymer served the cause from the beginnings of the movement for independence, although he never sought a public office in his life.

1739 Born Mar. 16 Philadelphia, Penn.

1757–58 Attended College of Philadelphia

1775–76 Treasurer of the United Colonies

1776–77 Member, Continental Congress

1780–82 Member, Congress of the Confederation

1784–88 Member, Pensylvania legislature

1787 Delegate to Constitutional Convention

1789–91 Member, U.S. Congress

1791–94 Chief U.S. Tax Collector in Pennsylvania

1795–96 U.S. Commissioner to Creek Indians

1813 Died Jan. 23 Morrisville, Penn.

17

JOHN DICKINSON

of

Delaware & Pennsylvania

"The Penman of the Revolution" was John Dickinson, who wrote many of the most influential documents of the period — from the Stamp Act Congress's *Declaration of Rights* (1765) and the Articles of Confederation (1776) to the Fabius letter, which helped win over the first States to ratify the U.S. Constitution — Delaware and Pennsylvania.

Having studied law in England, Dickinson was devoted to the British system of law *as it should work,* and his writings before 1776 aimed to correct the misuse of power and preserve the union of the colonies and Britain. His most famous writings were *Letters from a Farmer in Pennsylvania* (1768), which condemned the Townshend Acts and were widely read throughout the colonies; *Petition to the King* (1774), a statement of grievances and an appeal for justice, with a pledge of loyalty — which was adopted by Congress; and *Declaration on the Causes and Necessity of Taking up Arms* (1775). This Declaration, which Congress also adopted, defended the colonies' use of arms for "the preservation of our liberties," and stated that the colonists were simply fighting to regain the liberty that was theirs as Englishmen.

In the Continental Congress Dickinson opposed the idea of declaring independence, but, once it was done, he supported the cause and prepared a draft of the Articles of Confederation.

Although over forty, Dickinson enlisted in the militia and saw action in New Jersey and Pennsylvania. He returned to Congress in 1779, in time to sign the Articles of Confederation.

Because Delaware and Pennsylvania were under a single proprietor, a citizen could hold office in either one, and in the 1780s Dickinson served as President of first Delaware and then Pennsylvania.

By 1786 Dickinson was well aware of the shortcomings of the Confederation, and, as chairman of the Annapolis Convention, he was influential in planning the Constitutional Convention for the next year.

Dickinson played the important role of conciliator at the Constitutional Convention: he saw the need for a stable national government, and he joined Roger Sherman of Connecticut in supporting the idea of two legislative bodies — one with proportional (House), one with equal (Senate) representation — the Great Compromise that broke the deadlock between the large and small States.

After the Constitution was sent to the States, Dickinson published a series of letters, signed "Fabius," which explained and defended the Constitution, and which helped win the first ratifications — Delaware and Pennsylvania — in December 1787. The penman had done his work well: Jefferson called him "one of the great worthies of the Revolution."

1732 Born Nov. 8 Talbot County, Md.

1753–57 Studied law in England

1760–65 Member, Delaware & Pennsylvania legislatures

1765 Delegate to Stamp Act Congress

1770–76 Member, Pennsylvania legislature

1774–76 Member, Continental Congress

1776–78 Private—Brigadier General, Militia

1779–80 Member, Congress of the Confederation

1781–82 President of Delaware

1782–88 President of Pennsylvania

1783 Founder of Dickinson College

1786 Chairman of Annapolis Convention

1787 Delegate to Constitutional Convention

1808 Died Feb. 14 Willmington, Del.

19

BENJAMIN FRANKLIN

of

Pennsylvania

Patriot, inventor, scientist, philosopher, musician, editor, printer and diplomat, Benjamin Franklin brought the prestige of his unparalleled achievements to the public service that consumed over half of his life. He was the living example of the richness of life that man can achieve with the freedom — and the will — to do so. In many senses, he was the first American, and he was a Founding Father of the first rank.

Franklin's rise from apprentice to man of affairs was paralleled by an ever-widening circle of interests. His curiosity led him from subject to subject: he mastered printing, learned French, invented a stove, discovered electrical principles, organized a postal service, and helped discover the Gulf Stream.

As his country's representative in England in the 1760s, he defended America's position before hostile, arrogant officials; he helped win repeal of the Stamp Act and pleaded for American representation in Parliament. In the 1770s he continued to try to reason with British officials, but they were inflexible. He returned to America, ready to support the cause of independence.

In the Continental Congress Franklin headed the committee that organized the American postal system, helped draft the Articles of Confederation, and began negotiations with the French for aid. And he helped draft and signed the Declaration of Independence.

Franklin was the colonies' best choice as commissioner to France: well known as a scientist and philosopher, he was warmly welcomed in Paris, and his position as a world figure, coupled with his diplomatic skill, helped him negotiate the alliance with France (1778) which brought America desperately needed military support. Soon after, he began negotiating with the British for peace, but only after the French fleet had joined with Washington to defeat Cornwallis at Yorktown, would the British consider granting independence. Franklin signed the peace treaty September 3, 1783.

After he returned to America, Franklin had one more vital role to play: at the Constitutional Convention his very presence gave weight and authority to the proceedings, and he used his influence to moderate conflicts. On the final day he appealed to the delegates: "I confess that there are several parts of this Constitution which I do not at present approve, but I am not sure I shall never approve them. For having lived long, I have experienced many instances of being obliged by better information, or fuller consideration, to change opinions even on important subjects, which I once thought right, but found to be otherwise. . . . I cannot help expressing a wish that every member of the Convention who may still have objections to it, would with me, on this occasion, doubt a little of his own infallibility, and to make manifest our unanimity, put his name on this instrument." A few minutes later all but three delegates signed the Constitution.

BY JOSEPH WRIGHT

1706	Born Jan. 17 Boston, Mass.
1718	Apprentice printer
1723–	Printer, Philadelphia
1732–58	Publisher, *Poor Richard's Almanac*
1736–51	Clerk of Pennsylvania Assembly
1740	Invented Franklin stove
1752	Experiment with kite identified lightning as electricity
1753–74	Deputy Postmaster of colonies
1757–62	Pennsylvania representative in London
1764–75	Representative in London for Penn., Ga., Mass., & N.J.
1775–76	Member, Continental Congress
1776–85	Commissioner to France
1783	Negotiated peace treaty with Great Britain
1787	Delegate to Constitutional Convention
1790	Died Apr. 17 Philadelphia, Penn.

ELBRIDGE GERRY

of

Massachusetts

A patriot who signed the Declaration of Independence and the Articles of Confederation but refused to sign the U.S. Constitution, Elbridge Gerry worked vigorously for independence from the "prostituted government of Great Britain" yet feared the dangers of "too much democracy." At the Constitutional Convention Gerry refused to sign the Constitution because he could not accept the proposed division of powers or the absence of a bill of rights. Although he championed the people and their rights, he believed that the common man could be too easily swayed by unprincipled politicians for democracy to work. But he was not altogether consistent, for he was also jealous of power, fearful of possible tyranny.

Devoted to the patriots' cause in the early 1770s, Gerry was active as a member of the Massachusetts committee of correspondence and the first Provincial Congress. As one of the Congress's committee of safety, he was almost captured by British troops the night before the battles of Lexington and Concord. In the Continental Congress he supported the Articles of Confederation — with equal representation for all States, large and small.

Gerry represented his district in the first session of the U.S. Congress, but he refused to run after two terms. However, he was called to further service when, in 1797, President Adams selected him as a commissioner to France, along with John Marshall and Charles Pinckney, to attempt to improve U.S. relations with the revolutionary French government. French agents—identified as X, Y, and Z — insulted the commissioners by seeking bribes, and Marshall and Pinckney left. Gerry stayed and tried to negotiate with Talleyrand, but it is generally agreed that Talleyrand simply used Gerry by exaggerating the threat of war with the U.S. Upon his return, Gerry claimed credit for reducing the tensions between France and America.

As Governor of Massachusetts, in 1812, Gerry approved an unusual redistricting which favored his Democratic-Republican Party; one of the more extreme districts, shaped something like a salamander, was depicted by a cartoonist as a beast labeled "Gerrymander" — a term which has become a part of America's political language.

Gerry was elected Vice-President when Madison was elected to a second term in 1812, and Gerry was serving in his official capacity when he died suddenly. Ironically, he was riding to the Capitol to perform the duties of President of the Senate, a constitutional function of the Vice-President that he had objected to in 1787, and one of the reasons he had refused to sign the U.S. Constitution.

1744   Born Jul. 17   Marblehead, Mass.

1762   Graduated from Harvard

1772–73   Member, Massachusetts legislature

1774–75   Member, Provincial Congress

1776–80   Member, Continental Congress

1783–85   Member, Congress of Confederation

1786   Member, Massachusetts legislature

1787   Delegate to Constitutional Convention

1789–93   Member, U.S. Congress

1797–98   U.S. Commissioner to France

1810–12   Governor of Massachusetts

1813–14   Vice-President of the United States

1814   Died Nov. 23   Washington, D.C.

ALEXANDER HAMILTON
of
New York

Washington's most valued assistant in war and peace, Alexander Hamilton was probably the most brilliant writer, organizer and political theorist of the Founding Fathers. Time after time from 1776 to 1795 he brought his great powers of intellect to bear on the most critical problems facing the new nation — from obtaining a truly national constitution to establishing a sound national financial system.

Born in the British West Indies, Hamilton came to America at 17. William Livingston of New Jersey, who later joined Hamilton in signing the Constitution, gave the talented young man a home and sent him to college. By 1775 Hamilton had written two pamphlets defending the American cause which displayed an exceptional grasp of the principles of government.

During the war Hamilton distinguished himself in battle and served as Washington's aide. He organized Washington's headquarters and wrote many of Washington's statements and a complete set of military regulations.

An advocate of a strong central government, Hamilton led the delegates at the inconclusive Annapolis Convention to agree to meet in Philadelphia the next year "to take into consideration the situation of the United States, . . . to render the Constitution of the Federal Government adequate to the exigencies of the Union." His carefully worded proposal permitted more than it seemed to say: he opened the way for the Constitutional Convention. His influence was not so great at the Convention as after it, when he wrote 50 of the 85 Federalist Papers, which won necessary public support.

As first Secretary of the Treasury, Hamilton devised a comprehensive financial system which proved almost immediately successful: he proposed that the Federal Government assume the States' war debts, and, to settle these and foreign debts, that there be an excise tax, a national bank, and a protective tariff, which would also encourage American industry. The businessmen favored by these measures gradually grew into a political party under Hamilton. As first leader of the Federalist Party, Hamilton was, with Jefferson (of the Democratic-Republican Party), a founder of the two-party system — providing institutionalized rallying points for opposing points of view: Hamilton, who had little faith in the people, stood for an industrial society, a strong national government, and an aristocracy of power; Jefferson for an agricultural society, strong State government, and political democracy. Jefferson was more concerned with individual rights and freedom, Hamilton with governmental systems and procedures.

The Constitution and the Federalist Papers, the national financial system and the American two-party system — in a very real sense these are the legacy of the brilliant man who came to America a penniless youth.

1755 Born Jan. 11 Nevis, British West Indies

1773–75 Attended King's College

1776–77 Captain, Continental Army

1777–81 Aide-de-camp to General Washington

1782 Admitted to the bar

1782–83 Member, Congress of Confederation

1786 Delegate to Annapolis Convention

1786–88 Member, New York legislature

1787 Delegate to Constitutional Convention

1788 Member, New York Ratification Convention

1789–95 U.S. Secretary of the Treasury

1798 Appointed Major General, U.S. Army

1804 Died Jul. 12 After duel with Aaron Burr

JOHN HANCOCK
of
Massachusetts

Patriot, rebel leader, merchant — John Hancock signed his name into immortality in giant strokes on the Declaration of Independence on July 4, 1776, the boldness of his signature making it live in American minds as a perfect expression of the strength and freedom — and defiance — of the individual in the face of British tyranny.

As President of the Continental Congress, Hancock was the presiding officer when the members approved the Declaration of Independence, and, because of his position, it was his official duty to sign the document first — but not necessarily as dramatically as he did. (Only Hancock and the Secretary of Congress, Charles Thomson, signed the document at that time.)

Hancock figured prominently in another historic event — the battle at Lexington: British troops who fought there April 19, 1775, had known Hancock and Sam Adams were in Lexington and had come there to capture these rebel leaders. And the two would have been captured, if they had not been warned by Paul Revere.

As early as 1768, Hancock defied the British by refusing to pay customs charges on the cargo of one of his ships. One of Boston's wealthiest merchants, he was recognized by the citizens, as well as by the British, as a rebel leader — and was elected President of Massachusetts' First Provincial Congress.

After he was chosen President of the Continental Congress in 1775, Hancock became known beyond the borders of Massachusetts, and, having served as colonel of the Massachusetts Governor's Guards (1772–74), he hoped to be named commander of the American forces — until John Adams nominated George Washington.

In 1778 Hancock was commissioned Major General and took part in an unsuccessful campaign in Rhode Island. But it was as a political leader that he continued to serve — as first Governor of Massachusetts, as President of Congress, and as President of the Massachusetts Ratification Convention. He helped win ratification in Massachusetts, gaining enough popular recognition to make him a contender for the newly created Presidency of the United States, but again he saw Washington gain the prize.

Like his rival, George Washington, Hancock was a wealthy man who risked much for the cause of independence. He was the wealthiest New Englander supporting the patriotic cause, and, although he lacked the brilliance of John Adams or the capacity to inspire of Sam Adams, he became one of the foremost leaders of New England — perhaps, in part, because he *was* willing to commit a great fortune to the patriots' cause.

BY JOHN COPLEY   MUSEUM OF FINE ARTS, BOSTON

1737	Born Jan. 23 Braintree, Mass.
1754	Graduated from Harvard
1765–	Selectman of Boston
1766–74	Member, Massachusetts legislature
1774–75	President of Provincial Congress
1775–77	President of Continental Congress
1777–80	Member, Continental Congress
1780–85	Governor of Massachusetts
1785–86	Member, Congress of Confederation
1787–93	Governor of Massachusetts
1788	President of Massachusetts Ratification Convention
1793	Died Oct. 8 Quincy, Mass.

BENJAMIN HARRISON

of

Virginia

A wealthy Virginia planter and political leader, Benjamin Harrison risked his vast holdings along the James River by embracing the cause of independence from the time of the Stamp Act through the Revolution — and suffered severe losses during the war when British troops plundered his property.

While serving in the Virginia legislature, Harrison helped draft an official protest against the Stamp Act, and his activities as a member of the committee of correspondence and of the First Provincial Congress led to his selection as a delegate to the Continental Congress. There he served on three important committees, dealing with foreign affairs, the army, and the navy — the working committees that formed the nucleus of what later became major departments of the U.S. Government. Harrison also served in Congress as chairman of the committee of the whole, and, on July 2, 1776, he presided over the discussions that led to the vote in favor of Lee's resolution for independence. Harrison's signature on the Declaration of Independence is next to that of his fellow Virginian, Thomas Jefferson. In the Congress Harrison also presided over the debates that led to the adoption of the Articles of Confederation.

During the war Harrison served as speaker of the Virginia legislature and as Governor, the position he held when the British surrendered at Yorktown. While he was Governor, Virginia ceded to the Federal Government her claim to the lands north and west of the Ohio River, an action in which Jefferson played a major role, and one that helped strengthen the new Union.

As a member of the Virginia convention that met to consider ratifying the U.S. Constitution, Harrison was chairman of the committee on elections, but he did not participate in many debates; however, he joined Patrick Henry in refusing to support the Constitution without a bill of rights, and the absolute insistence of Harrison, Henry, George Mason and others to accept nothing less than a bill of rights did much to bring such provisions into the U.S. Constitution as the first ten amendments.

Of all the Founding Fathers, Benjamin Harrison is the only one who has the distinction of having two direct descendants — a son and a great-grandson — serve as President of the United States: William Henry Harrison, the ninth President, and Benjamin Harrison, the twenty-third President.

BY CHARLES PEALE

1726? Born — Charles City County, Va.

1745 Attended the College of William and Mary

1749–74 Member, House of Burgesses

1773– Member, Virginia Committee of Correspondence

1774–76 Member, Provincial Congress

1777–81 Speaker, Virginia legislature

1781–84 Governor of Virginia

1785–91 Speaker, Virginia legislature

1788 Member, Virginia Ratification Convention

1791 Died Apr. 24 Charles City County, Va.

29

PATRICK HENRY
of
Virginia

The most famous orator of the Revolution, Patrick Henry delivered dramatic speeches which kindled the spark of liberty in colonial Virginians and was, according to Thomas Jefferson, "far above all in maintaining the spirit of the Revolution."

In 1765, before the House of Burgesses, Henry spoke out boldly against the Stamp Act, firing the colony's opposition, and, in 1775, just weeks before Lexington and Concord, he closed a stirring appeal to arm the militia with the immortal "Give me liberty, or give me death!"

A failure as a farmer and storekeeper, at 24 Henry studied law and quickly won a reputation as a lawyer. In 1763, in the "Parson's Cause" case, he gained fame throughout Virginia by winning a point of law against the King's nullification of a Virginia law.

In the House of Burgesses in 1765, he responded to news of the Stamp Act by offering five daring resolutions that declared the colonists' rights, including the exclusive right to tax themselves, and he sought support with a fiery speech that evoked cries of "Treason." But Henry's powerful words helped stiffen resistance to the Stamp Act throughout the colonies and added to his reputation. In Virginia, he had more real power than the Governor.

At the First Continental Congress, Henry strongly supported the Continental Association, a union of colonies for the purpose of boycotting British imports.

It was at Virginia's revolutionary convention at Richmond that Henry, after proposing immediate arming of the militia, delivered the most famous speech of the Revolution, concluding, "Gentlemen may cry peace, peace — but there is no peace. The war is actually begun. . . . Is life so dear, or peace so sweet, as to be purchased at the price of chains and slavery? Forbid it, Almighty God! I know not what course others may take, but as for me, give me liberty, or give me death!" The convention promptly approved his proposal.

In the Continental Congress in 1775, Henry favored the idea of a Continental Army. No soldier himself (and his friend Washington agreed), Henry resigned a commission after a short time. As a member of the Virginia patriotic convention, he helped draft the State's constitution and bill of rights. He became Virginia's first Governor on July 5, 1776, and held the position for the legal limit of three years.

Although a leader of the Revolution, Henry was to the last a Virginian: when the Constitution came to Virginia for ratification, he fought it, believing it placed too much power in the Federal Government, depriving the States and the people of essential rights. And his fight against the Constitution and for the Bill of Rights, brought that issue to public notice throughout the colonies — contributing to the early adoption of the Bill-of-Rights amendments.

1736 Born May 29 Hanover County, Va.	1780–84 Member, Virginia legislature
1760 Admitted to the bar	1784–86 Governor of Virginia
1765–75 Member, House of Burgesses	1786–90 Member, Virginia legislature
1774–76 Member, Virginia Patriotic Convention	1788 Member, Virginia Ratification Convention
1774–75 Member, Continental Congress	1799 Died Jun. 16 Charlotte County, Va.
1776–79 Governor of Virginia	

JOHN JAY
of
New York

America's first Secretary of State, first Chief Justice of the Supreme Court, one of its first ambassadors, and author of some of the celebrated Federalist Papers, John Jay was a Founding Father who, by a quirk of fate, missed signing the Declaration of Independence. At the time of the vote for independence and the signing, he had temporarily left the Continental Congress to serve in New York's revolutionary legislature.

A conservative New York lawyer who was at first against the idea of independence for the colonies, the aristocratic Jay in 1776 turned into a patriot who was willing to give the next twenty-five years of his life to help establish the new nation. During those years, he won the regard of his peers as a dedicated and accomplished statesman and a man of unwavering principle.

In the Continental Congress Jay prepared addresses to the people of Canada and Great Britain. In New York he drafted the State constitution and served as Chief Justice during the war. He was President of the Continental Congress before he undertook the difficult assignment, as U.S. ambassador, of trying to gain support and funds from Spain.

After helping Franklin, Jefferson, Adams and Laurens complete peace negotiations in Paris in 1783, Jay returned to become the first Secretary of State, called "Secretary of Foreign Affairs" under the Articles of Confederation. He negotiated valuable commercial treaties with Russia and Morocco, and dealt with the continuing controversy with Britain and Spain over the southern and western boundaries of the United States. He proposed that the U.S. and Britain establish a joint commission to arbitrate disputes that remained after the war — a proposal which, though not adopted, influenced the government's use of arbitration and diplomacy in settling later international problems. In this post Jay felt keenly the weakness of the Articles of Confederation and was one of the first to advocate a new constitution. He wrote five Federalist Papers supporting the U.S. Constitution, and he was a leader in the New York Ratification Convention.

As first Chief Justice of the U.S. Supreme Court, Jay made the historic decision that a State could be sued by a citizen from another State, which led to the Eleventh Amendment to the Constitution. On a special mission to London he concluded the "Jay Treaty," which helped avert a renewal of hostilities with Britain but won little popular favor at home — and it is probably for this treaty that this Founding Father is best remembered.

1745   Born Dec. 12   New York, N.Y.

1764   Graduated from King's College

1768   Admitted to the bar

1774–77   Member, Continental Congress

1776–   Member, New York legislature

1776–79   Chief Justice, Supreme Court of N.Y.

1778–79   President of Continental Congress

1779–82   U.S. Minister to Spain

1782–84   U.S. Peace Commissioner in Paris

1784–89   U.S. Secretary of Foreign Affairs

1789–95   Chief Justice, U.S. Supreme Court

1794   U.S. Commissioner to Britain

1795–1801   Governor of N.Y.

1829   Died May 17   Bedford, N.Y.

THOMAS JEFFERSON

of

Virginia

The Declaration of Independence, the Virginia statute on religious freedom, the Northwest Ordinance — these documents are part of the legacy of Thomas Jefferson. In addition, he held almost every office in the land and, with Alexander Hamilton, created the American system of political parties.

It is almost impossible to estimate the ultimate value of these documents: the Declaration provided the intellectual and moral force for the American Revolution — and for others throughout the world; the statute on religious freedom established the principle of absolute separation of church and state; the Northwest Ordinance, which related to the Northwest Territory, guaranteed individual rights, prohibited slavery, and provided a formula for making and admitting new States on an equal basis with the old — principles that set the pattern for all future States.

Jefferson gained recognition as a writer and political theorist when his pamphlet, *A Summary View of the Rights of British America,* appeared in 1774. In Congress he was selected to draft the Declaration; in the Virginia legislature he helped draft 126 new statutes, including ones providing for public schools and libraries, which he believed necessary for an informed citizenry.

As minister to France, Jefferson negotiated trade treaties for the U.S. and won recognition as a political philosopher. During the Constitutional Convention he corresponded frequently with his disciple Madison, urging inclusion in the Constitution of republican principles and a bill of rights.

As Washington's Secretary of State, Jefferson and Hamilton, Secretary of the Treasury, became leaders of the first political parties. In the election of 1796, Democratic-Republican Jefferson was defeated by Federalist Adams, but Jefferson and his party won in 1800, a victory which marked the end of power for the Federalists.

In his inaugural address, Jefferson tried to heal the wounds: "We have called by different names brethren of the same principle. We are all republicans, we are all federalists." And, ironically, Jefferson as President in some ways acted like a Federalist, for this champion of State's rights who was always suspicious of centralized power, himself stretched the powers of the Presidency by buying Louisiana Territory, by sending Lewis and Clark to explore it, and by planning a federal system embracing roads and canals, arts and education. Jefferson's concern for the people was manifest in his belief in education and essential freedoms, and he turned the nation in the direction of democracy.

The range of Jefferson's interests is revealed in some of his other contributions — from the geometric shape of the western States to decimal coinage. And this universal man was so devoted to the principle of intellectual freedom that, as his epitaph reveals, he was as proud of founding a university as of founding a nation.

BY REMBRANDT PEALE   THE WHITE HOUSE COLLECTION

1743   Born Apr. 13   Shadwell, Va.

1762   Graduated from William & Mary College

1767   Admitted to the bar

1769–75   Member, House of Burgesses

1775–76   Member, Continental Congress

1776–79   Member, Virginia legislature

1779–81   Governor of Virginia

1783–85   Member, Congress of Confederation

1785–89   Minister to France

1790–93   U.S. Secretary of State

1797–1801   Vice-President of the United States

1801–09   President of the United States

1819   Founded University of Virginia

1826   Died Jul. 4   Monticello, Va.

WILLIAM JOHNSON
of
Connecticut

The only Founding Father who in 1776 was not in favor of independence, William Johnson grew into a strong supporter of the new nation: he helped draft the U.S. Constitution, signed it, and stoutly defended it at the Connecticut Ratification Convention.

Although he attended the Stamp Act Congress (1765) and served as a special agent for Connecticut in England (1767–71), Johnson during these years was firmly convinced that the colonies and Great Britain would settle their differences. His stay in London, where he associated with Dr. Samuel Johnson, the lexicographer, and other notables, undoubtedly strengthened his ties with England, although in London he worked closely with Benjamin Franklin, then agent for Pennsylvania and other colonies, in representing colonial interests. And he supported the American policy of non-importation of British goods as a protest against the Townshend Acts.

After returning, Johnson was elected to serve in the first Continental Congress, but since he was against the idea of independence, he declined the position. Still devoted to the idea of a peaceful settlement, in 1775 he visited the British commander, General Thomas Gage, in Boston — sent by the Connecticut legislature. His mission was unsuccessful, and he was for a time held by patriots there. He resigned from the Connecticut legislature, and from 1777 to 1779 his refusal to support independence cost him his law practice — which the State permitted him to resume after he swore allegiance to Connecticut.

Despite his tardy adoption of the cause of independence, Johnson was an influential member of the Congress of Confederation. At the Constitutional Convention Johnson, a soft-spoken but effective speaker, helped defend and explain the "Connecticut Compromise," the proposal for representing the States in the Senate and the people in the House of Representatives that was finally adopted — to settle the dispute between the large and small States. The scholarly Johnson, who was one of the colonies' leading classicists and who was then serving as president of Columbia College, was chairman of the committee on style that produced the final version of the Constitution (Committee-member Gouverneur Morris wrote most of it).

Johnson eloquently defended the Constitution at the Connecticut Ratification Convention, and, after ratification, Connecticut selected him to serve as one of the men to represent the State in the newly formed U.S. Senate.

1727   Born Oct. 7   Stratford, Conn.

1744   Graduated from Yale College
       (MA – 1747)

1749–   Lawyer

1765   Member, Connecticut legislature
       Delegate to Stamp Act Congress

1766–71   Member, Governor's Council

1774   Elected to Continental Congress;
       declined

1779   Arrested for treason; swore
       allegiance to Conn.

1785–87   Member, Congress of
          Confederation

1787   Delegate to Constitutional
       Convention

1787–1800   President of Columbia College

1788   Member, Connecticut Ratification
       Convention

1789–91   U.S. Senator

1819   Died Nov. 14   Stratford, Conn.

RUFUS KING

of
Massachusetts

For over forty years Rufus King served his country as a State legislator, member of Congress, delegate to the Constitutional Convention, U.S. Senator, Minister to Great Britain, and candidate for Vice-President and President. He helped draft both the Northwest Ordinance and the U.S. Constitution, which he signed and later supported at the Massachusetts Ratification Convention.

A student during most of the war, King began his public service as a member of the Massachusetts legislature, where he demonstrated his interest in the national cause by championing a bill that provided for regular financial support to the Congress of the Confederation. Later, while serving in Congress, he joined with Jefferson in contributing an anti-slavery provision to the Northwest Ordinance, the document that prescribed the conditions for the formation of new States from the Northwest Territory.

At the Constitutional Convention, where he was recognized as one of the most eloquent speakers, King maintained his position against slavery and supported the idea of a national government with clear authority beyond that of the States. As a member of the first U.S. Senate, the Federalist King supported the policies and programs of the nation's first administration. He backed Hamilton's financial plans and served as a director of the Bank of the United States, which he helped establish.

In 1796 he resigned from the Senate to become minister to Great Britain, a position which taxed his considerable diplomatic ability — helping to keep U.S. neutral while France and Britain were at war.

In the elections of 1804 and 1808, King was a Vice-Presidential candidate, running both times on the unsuccessful Federalist ticket with Charles Cotesworth Pinckney of South Carolina. In 1816 King was himself the Federalist candidate for President, losing to James Monroe. But King continued to serve in the U.S. Senate, where, in 1820, he opposed the Missouri Compromise — with the admission of Missouri as a slave state — as a failure to deal squarely with the problem of slavery. Forcefully but unsuccessfully, he advocated the abolition of slavery.

Handsome and sociable, King achieved success as a legislator and diplomat, and he won high praise as a speaker from one of America's most celebrated speakers. Of King, Daniel Webster wrote: "You never heard such a speaker. In strength, and dignity, and fire; in ease, in natural effect, and gesture as well as in matter, he is unequalled."

1755	Born Mar. 24 Scarboro, Mass.
1777	Graduated from Harvard College
1778	Aide-de-camp to General Glover
1780	Admitted to the bar
1783–86	Member, Massachusetts legislature
1784–87	Member, Congress of the Confederation
1787	Delegate to Constitutional Convention

1789	Member, New York legislature
1789–96	U.S. Senator
1796–1803	U.S. Minister to Great Britain
1804, 1808	Federalist candidate for Vice-President
1816	Federalist candidate for President
1825–26	U.S. Minister to Great Britain
1827	Died Apr. 29 Jamaica, N.Y.

JOHN LANGDON
of
New Hampshire

Builder of one of the first American warships, John Langdon was a wealthy merchant who gave freely of his fortune and himself in serving over thirty-five years in public office. Through those years Langdon showed an amazing willingness to serve the cause of the new nation however he could — as patriot leader, public official, soldier, shipbuilder and financier. Few other Founding Fathers gave themselves so totally to the cause.

Langdon led one of the first acts of outright rebellion against the British: in December 1774 he helped lead several hundred colonists on a raid on the royal fort in Portsmouth harbor in which they seized 100 barrels of British powder — and won fame throughout the colonies for their daring act.

While a member of the Continental Congress, he served on committees concerned with the purchase of military supplies, and he was appointed by Congress to build warships for a proposed navy. One of his ships, the *Ranger,* which was captained by John Paul Jones, was the first to fly the U.S. flag.

Langon was serving as speaker of the New Hampshire House of Representatives in 1777 when he learned of British General Burgoyne's march from Canada to try to cut off New England. New Hampshire planned to call out the militia but had no funds — so Langdon himself financed the State militia, and then fought with them in the battles of Bennington and Saratoga, two significant American victories.

In 1787, after Langdon and Nicholas Gilman were selected to represent New Hampshire at the Constitutional Convention, the State was again without funds — and Langdon paid the expenses of both delegates. At the Convention Langdon supported the idea of a new national government and, at the New Hampshire ratification convention, he adroitly managed to postpone the convention until ratification was assured. On June 21, 1788, New Hampshire ratified the Constitution; as the ninth State, it was the one that assured national ratification.

Langdon resigned from his second term as President of New Hampshire to become one of the State's Senators in the First U.S. Congress. As the first President of the Senate, he counted the electoral votes for President and informed George Washington of his election. He did, however, support Jefferson and his Democratic-Republican party during his twelve years in the Senate. After Jefferson was elected President, he offered the builder of those U.S. warships the position of Secretary of the Navy, but Langdon declined.

Returning to New Hampshire politics, Langdon served in the legislature and as Governor, but he was not completely forgotten by his party: in 1808 and 1812 he was considered as a candidate for the Vice-Presidency. But in 1812, after decades of service and generous support to State and nation, John Langdon retired from public life.

1741	Born Jun. 25 Portsmouth, N.H.
1775–82	Member, New Hampshire legislature
1775–76	Member, Continental Congress
1777–78	Captain — Colonel, Continental Army
1785–86	President of New Hampshire
1787	Delegate to Constitutional Convention
1788	Member, New Hampshire Ratification Convention
1788–89	President of New Hampshire
1789–1801	U.S. Senator
1801–05	Member, New Hampshire legislature
1805–09 1810–11	Governor of New Hampshire
1819	Died Sep. 18 Portsmouth, N.H.

RICHARD HENRY LEE

of

Virginia

Lee's resolution "That these United Colonies are, and of right ought to be, free and independent States . . . ," approved by the Continental Congress July 2, 1776, was the first official act of the United Colonies that set them irrevocably on the road to independence. It was not surprising that it came from Lee's pen: as early as 1768 he proposed the idea of committees of correspondence among the colonies, and in 1774 he proposed that the colonies meet in what became the Continental Congress. From the first, his eye was on independence.

A wealthy Virginia planter whose ancestors had been granted extensive lands by King Charles II, Lee disdained the traditional aristocratic role and the aristocratic view. In the House of Burgesses he flatly denounced the practice of slavery. He saw independent America as "an asylum where the unhappy may find solace, and the persecuted repose."

In 1764, when news of the proposed Stamp Act reached Virginia, Lee was a member of the committee of the House of Burgesses that drew up an address to the King, an official protest against such a tax. After the tax was established, Lee organized the citizens of his county into the Westmoreland Association, a group pledged to buy no British goods until the Stamp Act was repealed. At the First Continental Congress, Lee persuaded representatives from all the colonies to adopt this nonimportation idea, leading to the formation of the Continental Association, which was one of the first steps toward union of the colonies.

Lee also proposed to the First Continental Congress that a militia be organized and armed — the year before the first shots were fired at Lexington; but this and other proposals of his were considered too radical — at the time.

Three days after Lee introduced his resolution, in June of 1776, he was appointed by Congress to the committee responsible for drafting a declaration of independence, but he was called home when his wife fell ill, and his place was taken by Thomas Jefferson. Thus Lee missed the chance to draft the document, as he also missed the chance to vote, but he later signed the Declaration of Independence.

Elected to the Constitutional Convention, Lee refused to attend, but as a member of the Congress of the Confederation, he contributed to another great document, the Northwest Ordinance, which provided for the formation of new States from the Northwest Territory.

When the completed U.S. Constitution was sent to the States for ratification, Lee opposed it as anti-democratic. However, as one of Virginia's first U.S. Senators, he helped assure passage of the amendments that, he felt, corrected that — the Bill of Rights Amendments.

1732	Born Jan. 20 Westmoreland County, Va.
1747–51	Studied at Wakefield Academy, Yorkshire, England
1757	Justice of the Peace, Westmoreland County
1758–75	Member, House of Burgesses
1773	Member, Virginia Committee of Correspondence
1774–75	Member, Virginia Patriotic Convention
1774–79	Member, Continental Congress
1780–84	Member, Virginia legislature
1784–86	President of Congress of Confederation
1786–89	Member, Congress of Confederation
1789–92	U.S. Senator
1794	Died Jun. 19 Westmoreland, Va.

WILLIAM LIVINGSTON
of
New Jersey

A man with an abiding passion for justice, William Livingston used both the pen and the sword to fight tyranny wherever he found it: as a lawyer-writer in New York City he published essays attacking excesses of the Episcopal Church and the shortcomings of the legal profession, and as Brigadier General, he led the New Jersey militia during the first days of the Revolution.

As a youth Livingston displayed unusual talent as an artist, writer and linguist; at Yale he graduated first in his class. While studying law in New York City he wrote essays critical of lawyers for New York newspapers, the first of many essays and periodicals to come from his pen. In the 1750s he established himself as a lawyer and as a controversial writer. In a weekly, *The Independent Reflector,* Livingston, a Presbyterian, criticized the Episcopal Church for what he considered attempts to make it the established religion of the colony. In the following years he wrote a column for the New York *Mercury* called "The Watch Tower" (1754–55) and published *The Sentinel* (1765).

In May 1772 Livingston retired to an estate in New Jersey, and that October the 16-year-old Alexander Hamilton arrived with a letter of introduction from the Presbyterian minister who had helped finance his trip from the British West Indies. Livingston provided Hamilton the opportunity to attend school in Elizabethtown and King's College in New York.

As a member of the Continental Congress, Livingston followed a conservative course. In June 1776 he returned to New Jersey and assumed command of the militia, so that he was absent when the Declaration of Independence was considered and signed. Although some thought that Livingston was avoiding the issue, his brother Philip, from New York, *did* sign the Declaration.

After several months with the militia, Livingston was elected New Jersey's first Governor. Throughout the war he was forced to move about the State to avoid capture. He managed to elude the British, who destroyed his home, but he continued, in the face of great hardships, to support and direct the patriot's cause in New Jersey. The *Gazette* called him the "Don Quixote of the Jerseys."

During the war Livingston also wrote newspaper essays on patriotic subjects and against slavery. His influence was felt in the New Jersey legislature, which in 1786 prohibited the importation of slaves.

At the Constitutional Convention Livingston advocated equal representation of the States in the Senate; as Governor, he helped New Jersey become the third State to ratify the Constitution.

A devoted Federalist, Livingston lived to see Washington form the first government of the new United States, with the young man he had sent to college as the new President's principal domestic adviser, the first Secretary of the Treasury.

1723 Born Nov. 30 Albany, N.Y.

1741 Graduated from Yale College

1748 Admitted to the bar

1752–53 Published weekly, *The Independent Reflector*

1772 Retired from law practice

1774 Member, Committee of Correspondence

1774–76 Member (from N.J.), Continental Congress

1776 Brigadier General, New Jersey Militia

1776–90 Governor of New Jersey

1787 Delegate to Constitutional Convention

1790 Died Jul. 25 Elizabethtown, N.J.

JAMES MADISON
of
Virginia

One of the greatest of the Founding Fathers, James Madison earned the title "Father of the Constitution": he organized the interstate conventions at Mt. Vernon and Annapolis that led to the Constitutional Convention; he created much of the Virginia Plan, used as the basis for the final version of the U.S. Constitution, and contributed immensely to the Convention's success; he led the group that won ratification of the Constitution in Virginia; and he wrote Federalist Papers that lucidly explained the value of the system of government embodied in the Constitution. And in the First Congress he sponsored and obtained adoption of the Bill-of-Rights Amendments.

In the 1780s Madison recognized that the States must have a united commercial policy in order to deal effectively with foreign nations, and, not daring to hope for as much as a new constitution, he helped organize the interstate conventions at Mt. Vernon and Annapolis, which were to deal solely with commercial matters. At Annapolis, Madison, Hamilton and others were able to call for the convention in Philadelphia.

Several years before the Convention Madison began studying books on political philosophy and constitutional law that Thomas Jefferson sent him from Paris. He was well prepared to help draft the Virginia Plan, with its proposal for a truly national government. At the Convention he was clearly the best informed on political theory, and his vast knowledge, ready intelligence, and quiet reasonableness won him the respect — and the ear — of every delegate.

Besides taking the most complete notes of the proceedings of the Convention, Madison himself was involved in almost all deliberations of important points. With George Mason, Madison insisted that the people, rather than the State legislatures, must elect at least one branch of the national legislature — thus creating an entirely new political relationship that would give the citizen of every State direct representation in the national government.

More than any other man, Madison helped devise the unique division of powers between the national and State governments that was finally adopted. With a profound understanding of the needs of the States, he served as a moderating force between George Mason, the champion of individual liberty, and Alexander Hamilton, the champion of a strong central government. From the Virginia Plan to the Bill of Rights, no man contributed more.

Once the new government was formed, Madison continued to contribute: in the First Congress he helped prepare the legislation that established the departments of the Executive branch; in 1798 he wrote the "Virginia Resolution," which challenged the constitutionality of the Alien and Sedition Acts; as Secretary of State he was involved in the purchase of Louisiana Territory; and, as President, he led the nation through a war with England that cost him popularity but finally settled the question of American independence.

BY GILBERT STUART   COLONIAL WILLIAMSBURG

1751 Born Mar. 16   Port Conway, Va.

1771 Graduated from College of New
      Jersey

1776 Member, Virginia Convention

1778–79 Member, Governor's Council

1780–83 Member, Congress of
         Confederation

1784–86 Member, Virginia legislature

1786 Delegate to Annapolis Convention

1787 Delegate to Constitutional
      Convention

1788 Member, Virginia Ratification
      Convention

1789–97 Member, U.S. Congress

1799–1800 Member, Virginia legislature

1801–09 U.S. Secretary of State

1809–17 President

1836 Died Jun. 25   Montpelier, Va.

JOHN MARSHALL
of
Virginia

John Marshall is unique among the Founding Fathers: as a young officer in the Continental Army, he played only a minor role in the Revolution, and he did not contribute to, or sign, either the Declaration of Independence or the U.S. Constitution, but, as Chief Justice of the U.S. Supreme Court, he did more than any other man to stabilize the new national government by establishing the authority of the Court as co-equal with the Legislative and Executive, and by clarifying the fundamental relationship between the States and the national government. Contributions of such magnitude place John Marshall among the first rank of the nation's founders.

Although Marshall was only a junior officer in the Revolution (he fought at Brandywine, Germantown, and Monmouth, and endured Valley Forge), his experience in the war led him to see the need for a strong national government, for he realized that a stronger, better-organized government could have more effectively managed the limited resources available to the colonies to wage war. In addition, his military service provided the kind of experience that permitted him to think in *national* terms. Raised in the near wilderness of the frontier, Marshall, at age 20, was thrust into the world of the Continental Army: later he acknowledged that he became an American before he had had a chance to become a Virginian.

In the 1790s Marshall was well established as a leader of the Federalists in Virginia. He declined President Washington's offer of the position of Attorney General; he publicly defended the Jay Treaty; and in 1797 he was appointed by President Adams as a commissioner to France — for what became known as the XYZ Affair.

When Marshall was appointed Chief Justice, the Supreme Court stood far below the Executive and Legislative branches in power and prestige. By sheer force of intellect he produced decisions that won wide approval from constitutional lawyers, associates on the Court and eventually American citizens generally. He was so successful, so inevitably right in many of his views, that he *made* the Court the recognized interpreter of the Constitution. From 1801 to 1835 he delivered the opinion in over 500 cases, over 25 of which were fundamental constitutional questions.

Marshall's influence on our system was so great that the Constitution as we know it is, in large measure, Marshall's interpretation of it. A century and a half later, Marshall is still considered foremost of constitutional lawyers. According to a contemporary, Judge Jeremiah Mason, without Marshall's monumental efforts, the government of the new nation "would have fallen to pieces."

BY HENRY INMAN   PENNSYLVANIA ACADEMY OF FINE ARTS

1755	Born Sep. 14 Fauquier County, Va.	
1776–81	Lt. — Capt., Continental Army	
1782	Admitted to the bar	
1782–91 1795–97	} Member, Virginia legislature	
1788	Member, Virginia Ratification Convention	

1797–98	U.S. Commissioner to France	
1799–1800	Member, U.S. Congress	
1800–01	U.S. Secretary of State	
1801–35	Chief Justice, U.S. Supreme Court	
1835	Died Jul. 6 Philadelphia, Penn.	

GEORGE MASON
of
Virginia

Thomas Jefferson called him, "The wisest man of his generation," and this staunch defender of the rights of the individual, although he signed neither the Declaration of Independence nor the U.S. Constitution, was the source of some of the most revolutionary ideas in both of those documents. The drafters of both drew ideas from documents that were largely Mason's — the Virginia Declaration of Rights and the Virginia Constitution.

A Virginia aristocrat with a 5000-acre plantation, which he managed himself, Mason was a neighbor and friend of Washington. As a member of the House of Burgesses in 1769, Mason prepared resolutions against the importing of British goods, which Washington presented and the legislature adopted. In 1774 Mason wrote the Fairfax Resolves, advocating that all of the colonies meet in congress and that Virginia cease all relations with Britain. He was also primarily responsible for Virginia's relinquishing its claim to the lands beyond the Ohio River, the Northwest Territory, and he influenced Jefferson in his drafting of the Northwest Ordinance, with its prohibition of slavery and its provision for the formation of new States.

This Virginia planter played an unusual role at the Constitutional Convention, for he hated slavery, which he called "diabolical in itself and disgraceful to mankind," and he urged delegates at the Convention to give the new government the power to prevent the expansion of slavery. When the Constitution was completed, he refused to sign, partly because he felt the Constitution failed to deal strongly enough with the institution of slavery, permitting the importing of slaves until 1808, partly because it gave the Senate and President too much power and provided no protective bill of rights. He continued his opposition at the Virginia Ratification Convention, joining Patrick Henry, Benjamin Harrison, Richard Henry Lee and others who feared too powerful a central government. But Mason lived to see his most cherished ideas of the rights of the individual incorporated into the Constitution as the Bill-of-Rights Amendments in December 1791.

A rationalist who had little faith in the workings of governmental bodies, Mason fought passionately for the freedom of the individual — citizen or slave; and he was largely responsible for ensuring that protection of the rights of the individual would be such an essential part of the American system.

BY LOUIS GUILLAUME   VIRGINIA HISTORICAL SOCIETY

1725   Born — Fairfax, Va.

1749   Co-founder of Alexandria, Va.

1759–75 Member, House of Burgesses

1775   Member, Virginia Committee of
        Safety

1775–76 Member, Virginia Convention

1776–88 Member, Virginia legislature

1785   Delegate to Mt. Vernon Convention

1787   Delegate to Constitutional
        Convention

1788   Member, Virginia Ratification
        Convention

1792   Died Oct. 7   Gunston Hall, Va.

THOMAS MC KEAN

of

Delaware

Thomas McKean served in public office for over fifty years — the critical years during which the colonies moved toward revolution, the war was fought and won, and the new nation established. He held almost every possible position — from deputy county attorney to President of the Congress of the Confederation, the highest office in the land, and, besides signing the Declaration of Independence, he contributed significantly to the development and establishment of constitutional government in both his State and the nation.

At the Stamp Act Congress he proposed the voting procedure that Congress adopted: that each colony, regardless of size or population, have one vote — the practice adopted by the Continental Congress and the Congress of the Confederation, and the principle (state equality) manifest in the composition of the U.S. Senate. And as county judge in 1765, he defied the British by ordering his court to work only with documents that did *not* bear the hated stamps.

In June 1776, at the Continental Congress, McKean joined with Caesar Rodney to register Delaware's approval of the Declaration of Independence, over the negative vote of the third Delaware delegate, George Read — permitting it to be "The *unanimous* declaration of the thirteen united states. . . ." And at a special Delaware convention, he drafted the constitution for that State.

McKean also helped draft — and signed — the Articles of Confederation, and he served as the first President of the Congress of the Confederation. He was serving in this position in October 1781, when news arrived from General Washington that the British had surrendered. As Chief Justice of the supreme court of Pennsylvania, he contributed to the establishment of the legal system in that State, and, in 1787, he strongly supported the U.S. Constitution at the Pennsylvania Ratification Convention, declaring it "the best the world has yet seen."

At sixty-five, after over forty years of public service, McKean resigned from his post as Chief Justice. A candidate on the Democratic-Republican ticket in 1799, McKean was elected Governor of Pennsylvania. As Governor, he followed such a strict policy of appointing only fellow Republicans to office that he became the father of the spoils system in the U.S. He served three tempestuous terms as Governor, completing one of the longest continuous careers of public service of any of the Founding Fathers.

BY CHARLES PEALE

1734	Born Mar. 19 New London, Pa.
1754	Admitted to the bar
1756–57	Deputy Attorney General, Sussex County, Delaware
1757–59	Clerk, Delaware legislature
1762–79	Member, Delaware legislature
1765	Justice, County Court of Common Pleas
	Delegate to Stamp Act Congress
1772–73	Speaker of Delaware House of Representatives
1774–83	Member, Continental Congress
1777–99	Chief Justice, Supreme Court of Pennsylvania
1781	President of Continental Congress
1787	Member, Pennsylvania Ratification Convention
1799–1808	Governor of Pennsylvania
1817	Died Jun. 24 Philadelphia, Pa.

53

THOMAS MIFFLIN

of

Pennsylvania

By a twist of fate, Thomas Mifflin served as George Washington's first aide-de-camp at the beginning of the Revolutionary War, and, when the war was over, he was the man, as President of the Congress of the Confederation, who accepted Washington's resignation of his commission. In the years between, Mifflin helped the colonies' cause — and, quite frequently, his own cause — while serving as the first Quartermaster General of the Continental Army. He obtained desperately needed supplies for the new army — and was suspected of making excessive profit himself.

Although experienced in business and successful in obtaining supplies for the war, Mifflin preferred the front lines, and he distinguished himself in military actions on Long Island and near Philadelphia. Born and reared a Quaker, he was excluded from their meetings for his military activities.

A controversial figure, Mifflin lost favor with Washington and was part of the Conway Cabal, a plan to replace Washington with General Horatio Gates. And Mifflin narrowly missed court-martial action over his handling of funds by resigning his commission in 1778. In spite of these problems — and of repeated charges that he was a drunkard — Mifflin continued to be elected to positions of responsibility — as President and Governor of Pennsylvania, delegate to the Constitutional Convention, as well as the highest office in the land, President of the Congress.

Most of Mifflin's significant contributions occurred in his earlier years: in the First and Second Continental Congresses he was firm in his stand for independence and for fighting for it, and he helped obtain both men and supplies for Washington's army in the critical period — 1776–77. In 1784, as President of Congress, he signed the treaty with Great Britain which ended the war. Although a delegate to the Constitutional Convention, he did not make a significant contribution — beyond signing the document. As Governor of Pennsylvania, although he was accused of negligence, he supported improvements of roads, and reformed the State penal and judicial systems. Although he had become sympathetic to Jefferson's principles regarding State's rights, he directed the Pennsylvania militia to support the Federal tax collectors in the Whiskey Rebellion.

In spite of charges of corruption and of drunkenness, the affable Mifflin remained a popular figure. A magnetic personality and an effective speaker, he managed to hold a variety of elective offices for almost thirty years of the critical Revolutionary period.

1744 Born Jan. 10 Philadelphia, Penn.

1760 Graduated from College of
      Philadelphia

1772–75 Member, Pennsylvania
         legislature

1774–75 Member, Continental Congress

1775 Aide-de-camp to General
      Washington

1775–77 Quartermaster General,
         Continental Army

1778–81 Member, Pennsylvania
         legislature

1782–84 Member, Congress of
         Confederation

1783–84 President, Congress of
         Confederation

1785–88 Speaker, Pennsylvania legislature

1787 Delegate to Constitutional
      Convention

1788–90 President of Pennsylvania

1790–99 Governor of Pennsylvania

1799–1800 Member, Pennsylvania
           legislature

1800 Died Jan. 20 Lancaster, Penn.

GOUVERNEUR MORRIS
of
Pennsylvania

"We, the people of the United States, in order to form a more perfect union, establish justice, insure domestic tranquilty . . ." — famous words from the pen of Gouverneur Morris, who was primarily responsible for the final draft of the U.S. Constitution. He was also an eloquent, though sometimes windy, speaker, and members of the New York legislature, the Constitutional Convention, and the U.S. Senate were often swayed by his masterful blend of logic, wit, and imagination.

Although he had strong aristocratic tendencies, and as late as 1774 wrote, "It is in the interest of all men to seek for reunion with the parent state," in 1776 Morris spoke in the New York legislature on behalf of the colonies and against the King. He early recognized the need for a united, strong national congress. Of Morris, historian David Muzzey wrote, "he was a nationalist before the birth of the nation."

In the Continental Congress Morris was chairman of several committees, and his gifted pen produced such important documents as the instructions to Franklin, as minister to France, and detailed instructions to the peace commissioners, which contained provisions that ultimately appeared in the final treaty. As a member of Congress, he supported and signed the Articles of Confederation.

At the Constitutional Convention Morris participated in debates more than any other delegate. He argued that the President and the second branch of the legislature (the Senate) should be elected for life, and that the Senate should represent the rich and propertied, to counterbalance the democratic character of the House of Representatives. This was, of course, rejected, but his proposal for a Council of State led to the idea of the President's Cabinet, and he proposed that the President be elected, not by Congress, but by the people.

When the Constitution was completed, Morris was given the task of editing and revising it, and he then wrote the famous words of the preamble. Once the Constitution was formally accepted, Morris proved one of its most devoted supporters. On September 17, the day the delegates signed it, Morris made an impassioned speech answering Edmund Randolph, who refused to sign.

As U.S. minister to France in the 1790s, Morris found himself in the wrong country at the wrong time. Although he was recognized by the French revolutionists as one of the leaders of the American Revolution, he was nonetheless a Federalist with clear aristocratic sympathies. In Paris he became involved in attempts to help French nobles escape — including the Marquis de Lafayette and the King, and the revolutionists demanded his removal. After he returned he served in the U.S. Senate and, later, as chairman of the group that developed the plan for the Erie Canal, the waterway that opened the path for westward expansion.

BY ED. DALTON MARCHANT   INDEPENDENCE NATIONAL HISTORICAL PARK

1752	Born Jan. 31 Morrisania, N.Y.	
1768	Graduated from King's College	
1771	Admitted to the bar	
1775–77	Member, N.Y. Provincial Congress	
1776	Member, N.Y. Constitutional Convention	
1778–79	Member, Continental Congress	

1781–85   Assistant U.S. Superintendent of Finance

1787   Delegate to Constitutional Convention

1792–94   U.S. Minister to France

1800–03   U.S. Senator

1816   Died Nov. 6   Morrisania, N.Y.

ROBERT MORRIS

of

Pennsylvania

A Philadelphia merchant of great wealth who became the "financier of the Revolution," Robert Morris frequently risked his fortune on behalf of the Continental Army, was suspected — and cleared — of making excess profits on war supplies, and, near the end of his life, lost everything and spent three years in debtor's prison. With Roger Sherman, Morris shares the distinction of having signed all three of the principal founding documents — the Declaration of Independence, the Articles of Confederation, and the U.S. Constitution.

A conservative among the patriots, Morris did little besides sign a protest against the Stamp Act before he was elected to Congress in 1775, and he did not originally support the idea of independence, believing that the time was not ripe. He did, however, sign the Declaration — after he had abstained from the vote. And, in 1778, he signed the Articles of Confederation.

In 1776, as chairman of the executive committee of Congress, Morris was left in charge of the Government when Congress fled Philadelphia, then threatened by the British. Later that year Washington requested funds for an offensive, and Morris, pledging his personal credit, obtained the money that enabled Washington to defeat the Hessians at Trenton in December.

For the remainder of the war, Morris was, either officially or unofficially, the chief civilian in charge of finance and supply. In May 1781 Congress appointed him to the new position of Superintendent of Finance, and that summer he worked closely with Washington in planning the support for the major offensive against Cornwallis at Yorktown. Again Morris backed the purchase of ammunition and supplies with his personal pledge.

In 1779 a Congressional committee cleared Morris of charges that his firm was making excessive profits because of his position.

After the war Morris continued as principal finance officer for Congress, caught between the obligations of the Confederation and the States' continued refusal to support it. He all but exhausted his own credit and repeatedly planned to resign, but he stayed on. He established the first national bank, but Pennsylvania challenged its charter. By 1784, when he finally resigned, the United States had practically no credit abroad, and Morris urged the establishment of a stronger national government. At the Annapolis convention he supported the idea of the convention in Philadelphia. Host to Washington during the Constitutional Convention, Morris nominated Washington to preside and signed the completed document in September.

Morris declined Washington's offer of the position of Secretary of the Treasury in the new government and was elected one of Pennsylvania's first U.S. Senators. After he returned to private life he plunged boldly into land speculation and eventually lost his fortune. From 1798 to 1801 he was in Philadelphia's debtor's prison. He came out a broken and forgotten man.

BY CHARLES PEALE   INDEPENDENCE NATIONAL HISTORICAL PARK

1734 Born Jan. 31 Liverpool, England

1748– Studied in Philadelphia

1754–93 Partner, Willing & Morris Co., Philadelphia

1775–78 Member, Continental Congress

1779–81
1785–86 } Member, Penn. legislature

1781 Founded Bank of North America

1781–84 Superintendent of Finance, Congress of Confederation

1786 Delegate to Annapolis Convention

1787 Delegate to Constitutional Convention

1789–95 U.S. Senator

1798–1801 Imprisoned for debts

1806 Died May 8 Philadelphia, Penn.

CHARLES PINCKNEY

of

South Carolina

The "Pinckney Plan" of Charles Pinckney was one of the three plans offered to the Constitutional Convention in Philadelphia. No record of it exists, but Pinckney is generally given credit for many provisions (possibly over 30) of the finished Constitution. In an extremely active career, Pinckney also served as Governor of South Carolina (four times), U.S. Congressman and Senator, and U.S. minister to Spain.

Educated in England, Pinckney returned to assist — and then replace — his father (Col. Charles Pinckney) in South Carolina's patriotic movement. Before he was twenty he had served on the State's executive council and helped draft its first constitution. In the war he served with the militia, was captured, and spent a year in a British prison.

Elected to the Congress of the Confederation in 1784, Pinckney was in a position to be aware of the weakness of the government under the Articles of Confederation. As chairman of a Congressional committee considering measures to strengthen the Articles of Confederation, Pinckney gained experience which prepared him for his role at the Constitutional Convention; in 1786, in an address to Congress, he urged that a general convention be called to revise the Articles of Confederation.

When Pinckney arrived at the Constitutional Convention in Philadelphia in May 1787, he had already prepared his "Plan." Unfortunately he presented it to the Convention immediately after Edmund Randolph completed a three-hour description of *his* plan (the Virginia Plan), and the Pinckney Plan was never debated point by point, but simply referred, with other plans, to the committee on detail. And that committee did not identify, in its comprehensive report, the source of each recommended element of the Constitution. Though the exact extent of Pinckney's contribution to the Constitution remains unknown, Pinckney in later life made such extravagant claims that he became known as "Constitution Charlie." Pinckney also prepared a large part of South Carolina's new constitution, adopted in 1790 — a document modeled after the U.S. Constitution.

For more than thirty years after the U.S. Constitution was ratified, Pinckney served in public office. In the 1790s he left the Federalist party to support Jefferson: in 1795 he denounced the Jay Treaty, and in the 1800 election he helped Jefferson carry South Carolina, even though his cousin, Charles Cotesworth Pinckney, was the Vice-Presidential candidate on the Federalist ticket. President Jefferson's appointment of Pinckney as U.S. minister to Spain looked very much like a reward, but Pinckney had little success in dealing with Spain. After his return he continued to be elected to public office, completing his career in the U.S. Congress, where one of his final acts was to oppose the Missouri Compromise.

BY GILBERT STUART

1757 Born Oct. 26 Charleston, S.C.

1775–76 Member, Executive Council of South Carolina

1779–80 ⎫
1786–87 ⎬ Member, South Carolina
1805–06 ⎟ legislature
1810–14 ⎭

1779–81 Captain of Militia

1784–87 Member, Congress of Confederation

1787 Delegate to Constitutional Convention

1788 Member, South Carolina Ratification Convention

1789–92 ⎫
1796–98 ⎬ Governor of South Carolina
1806–08 ⎭

1798–1801 U.S. Senator

1801–05 U.S. Minister to Spain

1819–21 Member, U.S. Congress

1824 Died Oct. 29 Charleston, S.C.

61

CHARLES COTESWORTH PINCKNEY
of
South Carolina

"If I had a vein that did not beat with the love of my country, I myself would open it" — the sentiments of this Southern patriot who, though educated in England, was one of the principal Southern leaders of the new nation.

Charles Cotesworth Pinckney was twice the unsuccessful Federalists candidate for President — in 1804 against Jefferson and 1808 against Madison — but he is remembered primarily as a courageous Army officer, a signer of the U.S. Constitution, and as the U.S. commissioner to France who, in 1798, refused a veiled request for bribes with, "Millions for defense but not one cent for tribute." (Another version of his statement: "No, not a sixpence!")

After studying law under William Blackstone at Oxford, Pinckney attended the Royal Military Academy in France, gaining training which helped him, after he returned to America, to win a commission as a captain in the Continental Army in 1775. He fought in several battles and was captured when the British took Charleston in 1780. By the end of the war he was a Brigadier General.

Even before the war Pinckney was active in the patriotic movement. In 1775 he was a member of a group responsible for the local defense, and in February 1776 he was chairman of a committee that drafted a plan for the temporary government of South Carolina.

At the Constitutional Convention Pinckney stoutly defended Southern interests and State's rights; he revealed little faith in elections by the people, but he accepted the decisions of the convention, signed the Constitution, and supported it at the South Carolina ratification convention.

One of the most successful lawyers in South Carolina, Pinckney was offered a seat on the Supreme Court by Washington, but he declined — as he did later offers by Washington of the positions of Secretary of War and Secretary of State (1795). However, in 1796 he accepted the position of minister to France, but, after he arrived in Paris, the French Directory chose not to accept him, and he went to Holland. In 1797 President Adams appointed Pinckney, John Marshall and Elbridge Gerry commissioners to France — to attempt to settle differences, but the three were insulted by the French officials known as X, Y, and Z, and Pinckney made his famous reply and returned home something of a hero. He was soon appointed Major General in the newly formed U.S. Army, hastily organized by Washington because of the rupture with France, but by 1800 tensions were reduced.

Although he was twice unsuccessful in seeking the Presidency, Pinckney was honored by his fellow officers of the Revolution and served from 1805 until his death as president of their association, the Society of the Cincinnati.

1746	Born Feb. 25 Charleston, S.C.
1770	Admitted to the bar
1773	Assistant Attorney General of South Carolina
1775	Member, South Carolina Provincial Congress
1776–83	Officer, Continental Army
1787	Delegate to Constitutional Convention
1796	U.S. Minister to France
1797–98	U.S. Commissioner to France
1798–1800	Major General, U.S. Army
1800	Federalist candidate for Vice-President
1804, 1808	Federalist candidate for President
1805–25	President-General, Society of the Cincinnati
1825	Died Aug. 1 Charleston, S.C.

EDMUND RANDOLPH

of

Virginia

On May 29, 1787, Edmund Randolph introduced the Virginia Plan to the Constitutional Convention — the first time the idea of a new national form of government was formally presented to the delegates at Philadelphia. Although Madison contributed much to the plan, it was the handsome thirty-three-year-old Governor of Virginia, spokesman for his State, who began the Convention's serious deliberations by outlining the fifteen resolves that called for a national executive, judiciary and legislature. It was a dramatic moment: the delegates, officially gathered "for the sole and express purpose of revising the Articles of Confederation," were confronted with a radical proposal to create a completely different governmental system. That they heard Randolph out — for over three hours — and even considered the plan he offered, testifies to Randolph's success.

But Randolph was not pleased with some of the additions and revisions to the Virginia Plan that delegates introduced later, and he several times shifted his position, for and against; in September he refused to sign the final document. However, at the Virginia Ratification Convention, he shocked anti-Federalists like Patrick Henry by reversing himself and supporting the Constitution. Randolph explained his new position: by this time — June 4, 1788 — eight States had already ratified the Constitution, only one more was needed, and other States had already urged that bill-of-rights amendments should be enacted soon after ratification, satisfying Randolph's objection to the original Constitution. In a telling speech, Patrick Henry slyly suggested that perhaps there were other reasons — not going as far as mentioning a promised post in the new government, but the hint was enough: the two men came close to fighting a duel.

After Washington was elected President, he named Randolph the first United States Attorney General, but Randolph denied that this was in any way related to his supporting the Constitution. As Attorney General he established the office and the beginnings of the Justice Department, and after Jefferson resigned as Secretary of State, Randolph assumed that position also. In 1795 he was accused of seeking bribes from the French ambassador to the U.S., and though he proved himself innocent, he resigned and never held another public office.

1753 Born Aug. 10 Williamsburg, Va.

1775 Aide-de-camp to Washington

1776–86 Attorney General of Virginia

1779–82 Member, Continental Congress

1786 Delegate to Annapolis Convention

1786–88 Governor of Virginia

1787 Delegate to Constitutional Convention

1788 Member, Virginia Ratification Convention

1789–95 U.S. Attorney General

1794–95 U.S. Secretary of State

1813 Died Sep. 12 Clarke County, Va.

GEORGE READ
of
Delaware

Signer of the Declaration of Independence and the U.S. Constitution, George Read was one of Delaware's leading patriots — even though he did *not* vote for Lee's resolution to declare independence. Among the Founding Fathers, Read was a conservative rebel: in him the radical and conservative were so blended that he could refuse to vote for independence yet finally sign the Declaration and, at the Constitutional Convention, he could advocate the radical idea that the States be completely abolished, to ensure a strong national government, and yet approve the Constitution, with its complex federal-state system.

Known for his impartiality, thoroughness and judgment, Read won a wide reputation as a knowledgeable, effective — and honest — lawyer, and he was selected for almost every position that Delaware could give him. He devoted over thirty years to his State and nation — as colonial attorney general, legislator, convention delegate, State vice-president, State chief justice and U.S. Senator.

As early as the 1760s Read showed signs of being a cautious patriot — defending colonists' rights but avoiding radical positions. He supported the boycott of British goods and the idea of a Continental Congress. And the same year that he voted against Lee's resolution for independence and then signed the Declaration, he served as president of Delaware's constitutional convention and drafted most — perhaps all — of Delaware's first constitution.

At the Annapolis Convention in 1786, Read was one of those favoring a general convention at Philadelphia the following year. At the Constitutional Convention, he became known as an advocate of a strong national government. As a representative of a small State, he saw the complete elimination of the States as the best way to avoid having the large States dominate any form of federation, but this extreme idea was never seriously considered by the delegates. And he proposed that the Executive have the power to appoint the members of the Senate — another unusual proposal that found little support. However, after the Convention finally agreed on the substance of the Constitution, Read not only signed it, but also helped Delaware become the first State to ratify it.

As one of the first U.S. Senators, Read — a loyal Federalist — supported Washington's administration, and as chief justice of the supreme court of Delaware, he made decisions that contributed to the establishment of a sound system of law under the new Constitution.

1733 Born Sep. 18 Cecil County, Md.	1782–89 Judge, Court of Appeals
1753 Admitted to the bar	1786 Delegate to Annapolis Convention
1763–64 Attorney General for Delaware	1787 Delegate to Constitutional Convention
1765–80 Member, Delaware legislature	
1774–79 Member, Continental Congress	1789–93 U.S. Senator
1776 President, Delaware Constitutional Convention	1793–98 Chief Justice, Supreme Court of Delaware
1777–78 Acting President of Delaware	1798 Died Sep. 21 New Castle, Del.

BENJAMIN RUSH
of
Pennsylvania

"I was an advocate for principles in medicine," Benjamin Rush once said of himself. Actually he was a crusader for political and social, as well as medical, causes, a prolific writer, and a founder in all three areas: he signed the Declaration of Independence and supported the U.S. Constitution; he founded the first anti-slavery society and the first free medical clinic in America; and he wrote one of the first studies of mental illness and demonstrated his devotion to medicine by repeatedly risking his life caring for the sick during epidemics in Philadelphia.

Having studied on both sides of the Atlantic, Rush was one of the best educated physicians in America. By the 1770s he had won a place in Philadelphia as a teacher and a patriot as well as a physician. He was a friend of John Adams, Thomas Paine, and Thomas Jefferson, and, like them, an ardent champion of independence.

In 1773 Rush published a tract against slavery and the next year helped organize the Pennsylvania Society for Promoting the Abolition of Slavery, the first in America.

While his medical practice grew, Rush wrote newspaper articles for the patriotic cause and was elected to the Provincial Conference and signed the Declaration.

Strongly anti-royalist, Rush became suspicious of Washington's ambitions as commander-in-chief of the Continental Army and supported a secret movement, known as the Conway Cabal, to replace Washington with General Horatio Gates. Unsuccessful, Rush left his post as Physician-General in the Army and held no other Federal position until after Washington left the Presidency, when John Adams appointed him Treasurer of the U.S. Mint.

Rush's reputation as a physician and teacher grew with the years — although his medical "system" was challenged and later proven comparatively ineffective. He was a founder of the Pennsylvania Hospital and of the first free medical clinic for the poor. He became almost a legend as a professor at the University of Pennsylvania and as the saviour of Philadelphia during terrible yellow fever epidemics in 1793 and 1798. And he continued to write voluminously — defending the Constitution, helping James Wilson write the Pennsylvania constitution, producing his major medical books, and corresponding with his fellow patriots, John Adams and Thomas Jefferson. At the time of his death, Rush was probably the best-known physician in America.

BY CHARLES PEALE   WINTERTHUR MUSEUM

1745	Born Dec. 24 Byberry, Penn.	1777–78	Physician-General, Continental Army
1760	Graduated from College of New Jersey	1786	Founded first free medical clinic in America
1768	Graduated (M.D.) from University of Edinburgh, Scotland	1787	Member, Pennsylvania Ratification Convention
1769–	Professor of chemistry, College of Philadelphia	1791–	Professor of medicine, College of Philadelphia
1774	Founded first anti-slavery society in America	1797–1813	Treasurer, U.S. Mint
1776	Member, Continental Congress	1813	Died Apr. 19 Philadelphia, Penn.

JOHN RUTLEDGE
of
South Carolina

"Interest alone is the governing principle of nations," John Rutledge declared at the Constitutional Convention, in defending the South's "interest" in slavery. Gouverneur Morris called slavery "The curse of heaven," George Mason "this infernal traffic" — both wanted the Constitution to do more than ban further importation, but John Rutledge led the Southern opposition: the basic question, he said, was "whether the Southern States shall or shall not be parties to the Union." Faced with this challenge, the Convention chose to avoid the issue.

Like the Pinckneys, Rutledge studied in England and yet returned home a patriot. From the 1760s he was active in resisting British tyranny. At the Stamp Act Congress the 25-year-old lawyer, already a success in the courts of Charleston, denounced the British — and won recognition as a patriot and a forceful speaker. At the Continental Congress he worked to unite the disputing delegates, in order to present a common front against the British.

During the war Rutledge was President, and then Governor, of South Carolina, serving also as commander-in-chief of the State's militia. In 1776 he directed the successful defense of Charleston, with American forces driving off a British fleet, and in 1780 he helped win support for the forces that achieved an important American victory at King's Mountain.

At the Constitutional Convention Rutledge frankly defended slavery in the Southern States. "The people of these States will never be such fools as to give up so important an interest," he declared. And he maintained that wealth should be part of the basis for representation, and that the President should be elected by Congress, and Congress by the State legislature: he was not a champion of democracy or popular elections. As chairman of the committee of detail, Rutledge led the distinguished group that drafted the first version of the Constitution for the Convention. Although James Wilson and Edmund Randolph wrote most of it, Rutledge also contributed.

A product of the Southern plantation system, Rutledge is perhaps the best example of the eighteenth-century Southern aristocrat who could devote his efforts to the cause of independence from Britain and could strongly support the idea of a national union of States and yet flatly reject the political application, in *his* region, of the moral principle of freedom and liberty for all men.

1739 Born Charleston, S.C.	1784–91 Judge, South Carolina court
1761 Admitted to the bar	1787 Delegate to Constitutional Convention
1761–76 Member, South Carolina legislature	1789–91 Associate Justice of U.S. Supreme Court
1764–65 Attorney General, South Carolina	1791–95 Chief Justice of Supreme Court of South Carolina
1765 Delegate to Stamp Act Congress	
1774–75 Member, Continental Congress	1798–99 Member, South Carolina legislature
1776–78 President of South Carolina	
1779–82 Governor of South Carolina	1795 Acting Chief Justice, U.S. Supreme Court
1782–83 Member, Congress of Confederation	1800 Died Jul. 18 Charleston, S.C.

ROGER SHERMAN
of
Connecticut

A Yankee cobbler who taught himself law and became a judge and a legislator, Roger Sherman helped draft the three major American documents — the Declaration of Independence, the U.S. Constitution and the Bill of Rights. A signer of both the Declaration and the Constitution, he also helped draft and signed the Articles of Confederation, the nation's constitution from 1781 to 1789.

Sherman had almost twenty years experience as a colonial legislator behind him when he came to the First Continental Congress in 1774, and he quickly won the respect of his fellow delegates for his wisdom, industry, and sound judgment. John Adams called him "one of the soundest and strongest pillars of the Revolution."

In Congress Sherman was one of the first to deny Parliament's authority to make laws for America, and he strongly supported the boycott of British goods. In the following years he served with Jefferson and Franklin on the committee that drafted the Declaration of Independence, and on the one that drafted the Articles of Confederation. He also served on the maritime committee, the board of treasury and the board of war — all of first importance to the Revolution.

A Puritan of simple habits who performed all tasks with thoroughness and accuracy, Sherman gained more legislative experience in his years in Congress than any other member; by the time he left he was perhaps the most powerful — and most overworked — of congressmen.

Sherman's greatest contribution — and the best known — was the "Connecticut Compromise" he proposed at the Constitutional Convention: by proposing that Congress have two branches, one with proportional, one with equal representation, he satisfied both the small and the large States, providing a solution to one of the most stubborn problems of the Convention. In Connecticut he defended the Constitution, writing articles in the New Haven *Gazette*, and helped win ratification in January 1788. Connecticut was the fifth State to ratify.

Sherman was the oldest man elected to the new national House of Representatives. In the First Congress he served on the committee that prepared and reviewed the Bill-of-Rights Amendments. By coincidence, the year that the Bill of Rights became part of the Constitution Sherman was elected U.S. Senator — so that the man who conceived the "Connecticut Compromise" had the opportunity to represent that State in both of the legislative branches that he helped to create.

1721	Born Apr. 19 Newton, Mass.
1745	County surveyor
1754	Admitted to the bar
1755–61	Member, Connecticut legislature
1765	Judge, New Haven County
1766–85	Member, Governor's Council
1766–89	Judge, Connecticut Superior Court

1774–81	Member, Continental Congress
1781–89	Member, Congress of Confederation
1784–93	Mayor of New Haven
1787	Delegate to Constitutional Convention
1789–91	Member, U.S. Congress
1791–93	U.S. Senator
1793	Died Jul. 23 New Haven, Conn.

GEORGE WASHINGTON
of
Virginia

"First in war, first in peace, and first in the hearts of his countrymen," Henry Lee said of Washington, who, as a leader, also ranks first among the Founding Fathers. He led the make-shift Army to victory; he presided over the Constitutional Convention and helped bring the delegates from the thirteen states to unite under the Constitution; and, as first President, he translated the untried Constitution into the reality of an operating government.

From his early years Washington was strong, courageous, independent. At 16 he was surveying the western wilderness; at 22, he led a small band of militia who were defeated by a superior French force; at 23, as aide-de-camp to General Braddock, he demonstrated courage and poise under fire when a French ambush routed Braddock's troops. And as commander-in-chief of Virginia militia, Washington fought French and Indians on the frontier.

Washington attended the Virginia Patriotic Convention in 1774, where he offered to "raise one thousand men, subsist them at my own expense, and march myself at their head for the relief of Boston." Instead, he was chosen to go to the First Continental Congress; the next year Congress unanimously chose him commander-in-chief of the Continental Army.

Washington trained an army while avoiding confrontations with the superior British forces; he won occasionally with surprise attacks, but lost important battles at Philadelphia and Monmouth. In spite of inadequate suppliers, he held the army together through the lean years until the French provided support. With French and American troops, he planned and executed his greatest victory — over Cornwallis and some 7000 British regulars at Yorktown.

There were suggestions that the victorious General establish a monarchy, but Washington simply resigned and returned to Mt. Vernon. But his knowledge of the ineffectiveness of Congress convinced him that some other form of government was necessary, and he wrote leaders throughout the country advocating a change. He welcomed the Constitutional Convention, and as its presiding officer, he brought the prestige of America's war hero to the deliberations. He served as a moderating force through the debates, and his signature on the final document aided immeasurably in gaining ratification.

Washington was everyone's choice for President. He brought Jefferson and Hamilton into his cabinet, and his steady hand permitted the new government to grow amidst the conflicts of these two party leaders. After eight years, when he refused a third term, he had helped create the departments and traditions of the new republic. Although reserved and solemn, Washington embodied the essentials of the Constitutional Presidency, and he relinquished the power of the Presidency as firmly as he did that of the conquering General — another first, and one that set a compelling example for his successors. He had served his country mightily, winning a place among the world's great heroes.

BY GILBERT STUART

MUSEUM OF FINE ARTS, BOSTON

1732	Born Feb. 22 Westmoreland County, Va.	1775–83	Commander-in-chief, Continental Army
1749	Surveyor	1787	Chairman, Constitutional Convention
1752	Officer, Virginia Militia		
1755	Commander-in-chief, Virginia Militia	1789–97	President of the United States
1759–74	Member, House of Burgesses	1798–99	Commander-in-chief, U.S. Army
1774–75	Member, Continental Congress	1799	Died Dec. 14 Mt. Vernon, Va.

JAMES WILSON
of
Pennsylvania

"The best form of government which has ever been offered to the world," James Wilson called the U.S. Constitution, which he helped draft and later signed. He also signed the Declaration of Independence and served as Associate Justice of the first U.S. Supreme Court.

Although born and educated in Scotland, Wilson became a leader of the patriots as a young Pennsylvania lawyer. He studied law under John Dickinson in Philadelphia — and the two served in the Continental Congress together. In 1774, before he was elected to Congress, Wilson wrote a carefully reasoned pamphlet, *Considerations on . . . the Legislative Authority of the British Parliament,* which boldly concluded that Parliament had *no* authority over the colonies. In Congress he was one of three Pennsylvania members to vote for independence.

In a bizarre incident in 1779, Wilson's home was attacked by a faction of patriots who felt Wilson had betrayed the cause by defending in court merchants charged with treason. However, after the war he continued to represent Pennsylvania — in Congress and at the Constitutional Convention.

At the Constitutional Convention Wilson had a dual role — as a delegate and as spokesman for Benjamin Franklin, then 81. As a lawyer and political theorist, Wilson was deeply committed to the principle that sovereignty resides with the people, and he advocated popular elections for both the President and Congress. A member of the committee on detail, he wrote a draft of the Constitution which provided the basis for the final document, and throughout the convention he delivered the persuasive words of Franklin that moved the delegates to overlook minor differences and finally approve the Constitution. Later in 1787, at the Pennsylvania ratification convention, Wilson delivered a persuasive speech of his own, winning the votes necessary for ratification. Two years later his State called on him to draft a new State constitution.

During the first years under the new Constitution, Wilson served as an Associate Justice of the U.S. Supreme Court. One of his most significant decisions was his affirmation that the people of the newly formed United States formed a nation. And, as a lecturer in law at the College of Philadelphia, he undertook to translate the principle of the sovereignty of the people into the realm of law, providing legal justification for the Revolution and the beginnings of a uniquely American system of jurisprudence.

1742 Born Sep. 14 St. Andrews, Scotland

1763–65 Attended University of Edinburgh

1766– Classics teacher, College of Philadelphia

1767 Admitted to the bar

1774–75 Member, Pennsylvania Provincial Congress

1775–77 Member, Continental Congress

1779–82 Advocate General for France in America

1782–83 ⎫ Member, Congress of
1785–87 ⎭ Confederation

1787 Delegate to Constitutional Convention

1789–90 Member, Pennsylvania Constitutional Convention

1789–98 Associate Justice, U.S. Supreme Court

1798 Died Aug. 21 Edenton, N.C.

Signers of the Declaration of Independence

NEW HAMPSHIRE
Josiah Bartlett
Wm. Whipple
Matthew Thornton

MASSACHUSETTS BAY
Saml. Adams
John Adams
Robt. Treat Paine
Elbridge Gerry
John Hancock

NEW YORK
Wm. Floyd
Phil. Livingston
Frans. Lewis
Lewis Morris

NORTH CAROLINA
Wm. Hooper
Joseph Hewes
John Penn

SOUTH CAROLINA
Edward Rutledge
Thos. Heyward, Junr.
Thomas Lynch, Junr.
Arthur Middleton

NEW JERSEY
Richd. Stockton
Jno. Witherspoon
Fras. Hopkinson
John Hart
Abra. Clark

RHODE ISLAND
Step. Hopkins
William Ellery

DELAWARE
Caesar Rodney
Geo. Read
Tho. M'Kean

MARYLAND
Samuel Chase
Wm. Paca
Thos. Stone
Charles Carroll of Carrollton

CONNECTICUT
Roger Sherman
Sam'el Huntington
Wm. Williams
Oliver Wolcott

GEORGIA
Button Gwinnett
Lyman Hall
Geo. Walton

PENNSYLVANIA
Robt. Morris
Benjamin Rush
Benja. Franklin
John Morton
Geo. Clymer
Jas. Smith
Geo. Taylor
James Wilson
Geo. Ross

VIRGINIA
George Wythe
Richard Henry Lee
Th. Jefferson
Benja. Harrison
Ths. Nelson, Jr.
Francis Lightfoot Lee
Carter Braxton

Signers of the U.S. Constitution

NEW HAMPSHIRE
Nicholas Gilman
John Langdon

MASSACHUSETTS
Nathaniel Gorham
Rufus King

CONNECTICUT
William Samuel Johnson
Roger Sherman

NEW YORK
Alexander Hamilton

NEW JERSEY
William Livinston
David Brearley
William Paterson
Jonathan Dayton

PENNSYLVANIA
Benjamin Franklin
Thomas Mifflin
Robert Morris
George Clymer
Thomas Fitzsimons
Jared Ingersoll
James Wilson
Gouverneur Morris

DELAWARE
George Reed
Gunning Bedford, Junior
John Dickinson
Richard Bassett
Jacob Broom

MARYLAND
James McHenry
Daniel of St. Tho. Jenifer
Daniel Carrol

VIRGINIA
John Blair
James Madison, Junior

NORTH CAROLINA
William Blount
Richard Dobbs Spaight
Hugh Williamson

SOUTH CAROLINA
John Rutledge
Charles Cotesworth Pinckney
Charles Pinckney
Pierce Butler

GEORGIA
William Few
Abraham Baldwin

Acknowledgements

For assistance in obtaining the portraits of the Founding Fathers, I am indebted to:

Mr. David McIntyre, Baltimore Museum of Art
Miss Elaine Zetes, Museum of Fine Arts, Boston
Miss Elizabeth Rodgers, Colonial Williamsburg
Mr. Glenn Thomas, Corcoran Gallery of Art
Miss Mildred Steinbach, Miss Helen Sanger, Mr. Gregory Jedzinak and Mr. Eliot Rowlands, Frick Art Reference Library
Mr. Robert Giannini, Mr. Warren McCullough, Independence National Historical Park
Mr. Anthony Cucchiara, Long Island Historical Society
Mrs. Lois McCauley, Mrs. Katy Thomas, Maryland Historical Society
Mr. Monroe Fabian, Mrs. Ethel Newell, National Portrait Gallery
Mr. James Heslin, New-York Historical Society
Mrs. Mary Southall, Virginia Historical Society
Miss Karol Schmiegel, Winterthur Museum
Miss Susan Ewell, The White House
Miss Denise D'Avella, Yale University Art Gallery

For assistance and advise, I am indebted to:

Dr. Robert F. Brockmann of the University of Maryland
Mr. Robert Kramer, Mr. James Quinn of R. R. Donnelley & Sons Co.
Mrs. Brenda Smith of Glen Burnie, Maryland

A teacher, writer and editor, Mr. Wilson is the author of *The Book of the Presidents* and *The Book of the States,* and editor of *The Book of Great American Documents.* The latter two have been selected for awards by the Freedoms Foundation at Valley Forge. A native of Cleveland, Mr. Wilson studied at Georgetown, Arizona State, Claremont and Harvard.

COVER: The Declaration of Independence by John Trumbull
COURTESY CAPITOL HISTORICAL SOCIETY